PRAYING WITH
THE ORTHODOX TRADITION

PRAYING WITH
The Orthodox Tradition

Compiled by
Stefano Parenti

Translated by
Paula Clifford

Preface by
Bishop Kallistos Ware

First published 1989
Triangle
SPCK
Holy Trinity Church
Marylebone Road
London NW1 4DU

British Library Cataloguing in Publication Data

Parenti, Stefano
Praying with orthodox tradition.
1. Orthodox Eastern Church. Christian life.
Prayer
I. Title   II. Signore della gloria. *English*
248.3'2

ISBN 0-281-04431-7

Typeset by Rowland Phototypesetting Ltd
Bury St Edmunds, Suffolk
Printed in Great Britain by
BPCC Hazell Books Ltd
Member of BPCC Ltd
Aylesbury, Bucks, England

Contents

Preface

'Remember God more often than you breathe', says St Gregory of Nazianzus (d. 389). Prayer is more essential to us, more an integral part of ourselves, than the rhythm of our breathing or the beating of our heart. Without prayer there is no life. Prayer is our nature. As human persons we are created for prayer just as we are created to speak and to think. The human animal is best defined, not as a logical or tool-making animal or an animal that laughs, but rather as an animal that prays, a eucharistic animal, capable of offering the world back to God in thanksgiving and intercession.

If, then, we wish to understand the members of any religious community not our own, whether Christian or non-Christian, the most helpful means of approach is to look at their experience of prayer. What is their sense of the sacred? How do they invoke the Spirit? What use do they make of symbol and sacrament, of word and silence, as they stand before God? The ecumenical quest is above all else the mutual discovery of our ways of prayer. This present volume, *Praying with the Orthodox Tradition*, deserves therefore a warm and wide welcome. I am confident that it will make the Christian East better known and loved.

The liturgical worship of the Orthodox Church is extraordinarily rich and varied, and it would be altogether impossible for a short anthology such as this to include every aspect. Stefano Parenti has wisely chosen to limit his selection to a particular theme. Basing himself on one of the most ancient of Greek liturgical manuscripts, the Barberini Codex 336, dating from the late eighth century, he has chosen from it the prayers said by the celebrant during the twenty-four hour cycle of the daily services. We have here prayers for sunset, night prayers before retiring to bed, prayers for midnight and dawn, prayers for early and mid morning, for midday and the afternoon. So we are shown how Christ, the maker and Lord of time, can be brought into all the different moments of our day. The book reveals to us time transfigured – time assumed into God, renewed, sanctified.

For many centuries unfortunately it has been the practice in the Orthodox Church for the officiating priest to recite these prayers in a low voice, inaudible to the congregation, whereas they ought in fact to be said aloud in the hearing of all. This means that today they are little known to most of the Orthodox laity. Moreover, the Barberini Codex provides a far fuller series of prayers than can be found in the modern printed service books. Thus, for Orthodox no less than Western Christians, this present collection contains much that will be refreshingly new.

Presupposed by the prayers that follow is a basic scheme of six services performed in each period of twenty-four hours (see the editor's appendix for fuller details). Since the time of the Barberini Codex two further services have been added, and so the present-day sequence runs:

Vespers (at sunset)
The 'after-supper service' or Compline (before going to sleep)
The Midnight Office
Matins or Orthros (at dawn)
The first hour or Prime (around 7.00 a.m.)
The third hour or Terce (9.00 a.m.)
The sixth hour or Sext (at noon)
The ninth hour or None (3.00 p.m.)

Sometimes a vigil (*agrypnia*, *pannychis*) is held during part or all of the night, while at certain seasons of the year there are also short intermediate services appointed for the morning and afternoon, known as the 'Inter-Hours'. The full cycle is now observed only in the monasteries, but most parish churches in

Greece and Russia still celebrate daily the two chief services in the sequence, Vespers and Matins.

The daily cycle commences at Vespers. The Orthodox Church, following the ancient Jewish understanding of time, regards the new day as commencing not at midnight or at dawn but at sunset. 'And there was evening and there was morning, one day' (Genesis 1.5): each of the six days of creation begins in the biblical account with the evening, not the morning. The prayers of Vespers are not the last but the first act of worship in the day, not an epilogue but a fresh start. That is why they emphasise in particular the theme of creation: at the beginning of each new day, we call to mind the beginning of the world. But, since for the modern reader it might seem strange to end our daily worship with prayers for the afternoon, Stefano Parenti has placed at the end of the selection some of the night-time prayers used at the *pannychis* or vigil.

Prominent throughout the daily prayers of the Orthodox Church is the theme of light, understood both as a physical reality and as a symbol. The alternation of daylight and darkness is the primary way in which we experience the passing of time. So the prayers bless God who 'separates light from darkness', who 'made the sun to give light to the day and brightened the night with shining stars'. Light is evoked in its many variations: the gentle light of evening, the light of dawn 'shining out of darkness', the full sunlight of midday. Ascending from the physical to the spiritual level, we invoke God 'the eternal light that never grows dim', who 'dwells in light unapproachable' (1 Timothy 6.16), and we welcome Christ incarnate as the light of the world.

The prayers also connect the different moments of the day with events in the history of salvation. The third hour is linked with the outpouring of the Holy Spirit on the day of Pentecost (Acts 2.15), noon with the nailing of the Saviour to the Cross (Luke 23.44) and with Peter's prayer on the housetop at midday (Acts 10.9), the ninth hour with Christ's death on the Cross (Mark 15.34) and with the miraculous healing of the lame man by Peter and John in the temple (Acts 3.1). Time is in this way taken up into God's saving action and experienced, not as loss or meaningless repetition, but as sacred and redeeming time, *kairos*, the moment of truth and opportunity.

Inevitably the plan adopted by Stefano Parenti has meant that many themes, of fundamental importance to the Orthodox worshipper, cannot be represented here. The book does not include any texts from the Church's year, the annual cycle of feasts and fasts centred upon Easter and Christmas. Likewise it does not contain prayers for baptism, the eucharist, marriage and the other sacraments. Also outside its scope are countless prayers used by Orthodox Christians for the sick and the dying, and for special needs and familiar daily tasks. Orthodoxy recognises no sharp distinction between the sacred and the secular; every aspect of our daily life and work is blessed by the Church and so brought within the realm of divine grace. As Christians we are necessarily materialists; ours is an incarnate faith, earthy, rooted in this world. Thus our Orthodox service books contain prayers for sowing, threshing and wine-making, for diseased sheep or cattle, for blessing cars, tractors and fishing-nets, for insomnia, for children starting to learn the alphabet or students taking their examinations. In the older editions there are even rites for cursing caterpillars and removing dead rats from the bottom of a well. Jesus Christ at his human birth took upon him our whole nature – body, soul and spirit – and so he is rightly involved in everything that we do. We meet him everywhere.

Within its carefully chosen limits, however, the present book illustrates many of the dominant characteristics of Orthodox worship. First of all, the prayers are profoundly biblical, filled with phrases and images taken directly from Scripture. Orthodox Christians, no less than Western Protestants, see themselves as 'evangelicals', members of a Church that is founded on the Bible. In the words of a great Russian Orthodox theologian of the nineteenth century, Metropolitan Philaret of Moscow, 'The only pure and all-sufficient source of the doctrines of the faith is the revealed word of God.'

Four other themes recur constantly in the pages that follow. First, the prayers are marked by a strong sense of God's holiness and mystery, by a spirit of reverence and wonder. We approach the living God 'in fear and trembling', 'in love and awe'. Negative or apophatic language is used to underline the divine transcendence: God's power is 'indescribable' and his goodness 'unutterable'; 'your glory cannot be approached . . . no one has ever seen you nor is able to see you . . . who alone are holy, immeasurable and beyond human expression . . . incomprehensible in being'. Such language, so far from being an empty formality, expresses a vivid, inescapable conviction pervading all Orthodox theology. Yet Orthodoxy feels the nearness as well as the otherness of God. Transcendent, ineffable, he is also at the core of everything, closer to us than our own heart, 'everywhere present and filling all things', as we say to the Holy Spirit in an invocation at the start of each service.

Secondly, Orthodox worship is deeply Trinitarian. 'Between the Trinity and hell there lies no other choice', says the Russian theologian Vladimir Lossky. The threefold invocation, 'Father, Son and Holy Spirit', with which each prayer concludes, is not an optional extra but sums up the very essence of our prayer. We do not simply address God, but explicitly or implicitly we always pray *to* the Father, *through* the Son, *in* the Spirit. To pray is to be taken up into a network of relationships, an interpersonal dialogue, that exists within God himself. As we pray, we hear the Father say not to Christ only but also to ourselves, 'You are my beloved Son' (Mark 1.11); and by the power of the Spirit we respond in union with Christ, 'Abba, Father' (Romans 8.15; Galatians 4.6), becoming sons in the Son. So through prayer we are assumed into the *perichoresis*, the mutual love or 'round dance' of the Trinity. God as Trinity is the source and end-point of all our prayer.

In the third place, all prayer is communal – prayer of the total family, of the entire Church invisible as well as visible. Prayer is our entry to the communion of saints. Even when praying in secret with the door closed (Matthew 6.6), we are never praying alone. In the Lord's Prayer the words 'our' and 'us' occur each four times, whereas 'mine' and 'me' are never used at all. The Christian is the one who says not 'I' but 'we'; and this 'we', in the Orthodox tradition, embraces not just the members of the visible congregation but the saints, the angels, the Blessed Virgin Mary. Prayer is 'heaven on earth'. This does not diminish the love that we feel for Christ our only Saviour, 'the one mediator between God and humans' (1 Timothy 2.5), but renders him all the closer to us.

Fourthly and finally, in prayer we do not think only in vertical terms about the Church in glory and the communion of saints, but we also think horizontally about our involvement with the rest of humankind. This is evident, for example, in the prayers said for the catechumens, the new converts who are shortly to receive baptism: 'Pour your Holy Spirit upon them that they too may become the little sheep of the one true shepherd . . . Grant them new birth from the waters of baptism.' Such prayers are not just a survival from the past, an archaeological relic, but form an all-important reminder that the Church is by its very nature missionary, outward-looking, existing not for itself but for the sake of the world. This missionary commitment of the Church is something that we Orthodox are all too often in danger of forgetting. If within our congregations there are actually no such catechumens, no adults preparing for Christian 'illumination', then instead of omitting these prayers as irrelevant let us rather ask ourselves why the sense of mission is so sadly absent from our religious outlook.

'Pray without ceasing', says St Paul (1 Thessalonians 5.17); and the Russian Orthodox Fr Georges Florovsky writes: 'A Christian has to feel himself personally in the presence of God. The goal of prayer is precisely to be with God always.' I hope that the prayers in this book, designed for the different hours of the day, will help us in small but significant ways to do exactly that: to be with God always, to make our prayer, not just an intermittent activity, but a dimension present continually in all that we undertake – not simply something that we *do* from time to time, but something that we *are* the whole time. For this is what the world around us needs: not that we should say prayers occasionally, but that we should be at each moment a living flame of prayer.

BISHOP KALLISTOS OF DIOKLEIA

Introduction

1988 saw the solemn celebration of the millenium of the Russian Church. Its glorious yet tormented history is traditionally said to have begun in 988 when, on the banks of the river Dnieper, missionaries from Constantinople baptised Prince Vladimir, and all Russia with him, into the Christian faith.

That story is little more than a legend. Yet it might well have been the splendour of the Byzantine liturgy that led to Russia adopting Christianity in the form in which it was expressed at New Rome. Vladimir, so the story goes, sent his envoys across Europe to observe different religions in order that he might choose one for his people.

His ten envoys first encountered the Bulgars (Muslims) who made an unfavourable impression; next they met the Germans (Catholics) and then headed for Constantinople, where they were fortunate enough to attend a service celebrated by the Patriarch himself. Returning to their own country they reported the end of their travels to Vladimir as follows:

> The Greeks led us to the edifices where they worship their God, and we knew not whether we were in heaven or on earth. For on earth there is no such splendour or such beauty, and we are at a loss how to describe it. We only know that God dwells there among men . . . we cannot forget that beauty. Every man, after tasting something sweet, is afterwards unwilling to accept that which is bitter . . .[1]

Historical accuracy aside, there clearly emerges from these lines a crucial aspect of the development of Byzantine liturgical prayer: the importance of beauty or the 'aesthetics of worship', which may be seen in various contemporary writers.[2] However, without wishing to detract in any way from these 'outward' appearances, which are an integral part of liturgical language, we must never lose sight of the structures underlying them, and these are represented by the *euchologion* or heritage of prayers established by tradition. This tradition is a clear and unequivocal expression of how a Church perceives, *lives* and celebrates the Mystery of Christ in its own life. The liturgy, according to a highly felicitous definition in the *sacramentarium* of Verona, is none other than the place where 'the work of our redemption is accomplished' and made manifest.[3]

Compiling an anthology of Byzantine liturgical prayers out of the huge amount of material available poses a number of problems as to which to choose. It should also be remembered that the present collection is not the first of its kind.

In order to avoid any possible misunderstanding or unnecessary duplication, we have decided first and foremost to remain faithful to the general title of the series. We are therefore including only prayers and not other forms of liturgical composition. Many anthologies of Byzantine prayers have in fact been produced which on closer examination turn out to be collections of liturgical *poetry*.

Thanks to the strong lead given by Vatican Council II, the Christian West is at present increasingly rediscovering the community dimension of prayer and is emerging from its ancient tunnel of private devotions. This, then, seems to be a particularly appropriate time to bring to readers' attention the prayers of the ancient Liturgy of the Hours of the cathedral of Byzantium, the 'Great Church', many of which have fallen into disuse.

The *euchologion*, like the writings of the Fathers and like Holy Scripture itself, has been handed down in a manuscript tradition. We have therefore based our translation wholly on the oldest extant form of the Byzantine liturgy, the Codex *Barberini gr 336* that dates from the end of the 8th Century. This choice is not dictated by archaeological considerations; rather, it is part of the rediscovery of a 'global tradition' that transcends the limits of the texts as we know them from today's liturgical books, which are not generally compiled according to any critical criterion. It is a choice that seeks to be like that of the house owner who brings out of his store room, in this case the store room of the whole Church, new treasures as well as old (Matthew 13.52).

We have included as an appendix a study which, without pretending to be exhaustive, may serve as an introduction to the Byzantine liturgical *kosmos*. This is intended to help the reader towards a better understanding of the *euchologion* texts reproduced here: their sources, the structures in which they occur, and the themes that underlie the various prayers.

Finally we should like to thank the many people who have helped in and supported the compilation of this book. The most appropriate expression of our gratitude may perhaps be found in the words of the Eucharistic prayer attributed to Basil of Caesarea who died in 379:

> Remember, O Lord, those whom we have omitted through ignorance, forgetfulness
> or because of the sheer number of their names . . .
> you who know the needs and situation of each one of them.[4]

Notes
1 *The Russian Primary Chronicle*, translated and edited by S. H. Cross and O. P. Sherbowitz-Wetzor, (Cambridge, Mass), pages 110–111.
2 See especially G. P. Fedotov, *The Russian Religious Mind*, (Cambridge 1946–60), I.371; II.355.
3 *Sacramentarium Veronese*, edited by L. C. Mohlberg, L. Eizenhofer, P. Siffrin, (Rome 1956), page 93.
4 *Euchologion to mega*, (Rome 1873) page 97.

WELCOME CHRIST, THE TRUE LIGHT

Sunset

(Vespers)

May my prayer be set before you
like incense;
may the lifting up of my hands be
like the evening sacrifice
Psalm 141.2 NIV

O Lord,
physician and healer of our souls,
do not rebuke us in your displeasure
nor punish us in your wrath,
but deal with us according to your mercy.
Guide us into the haven of your will,
enlighten our hearts
with the knowledge of your truth,
and grant that the rest of this day
and the remainder of our lives
may pass in peace and without sin;
we ask this
through the mediation of the holy Mother of God
and all the saints.

For yours, Lord, is the greatness and the majesty,
the power and the glory,
Father, Son and Holy Spirit,
now and for ever,
to the ages of ages.   Amen.

Psalm 6.1–2. Psalm 38.1. Psalm 107.30. Ephesians 1.18.
Hebrews 10.26.

O Lord our God,
remember us sinners, your helpless servants,
as we call upon your holy and blessed Name.
Let us not wait in vain for your mercy,
but in your goodness, O Lord,
grant us what we ask, that we may be saved:
may we love and fear you
with all our hearts
and in everything do your will.

For you, O God,
are good and loving to everyone
and we glorify you,
Father, Son and Holy Spirit,
now and for ever,
to the ages of ages.   Amen.

Psalm 74.2. Psalm 116. Deuteronomy 6.5

Around your throne in heaven
angelic powers exalt you
with ceaseless hymns
and unending songs of praise;
so may your praise be ever on our lips
that we may proclaim
the greatness of your holy Name.
Grant that we may
share in the inheritance you have promised us,
together with all those who hear you, who walk in your
    truth
and obey your commandments;
we ask this
through the mediation of the holy Mother of God
and all the saints.

Through the great goodness
of your only-begotten Son
who with you and your most holy
and life-giving Spirit
is to be praised
now and for ever,
to the ages of ages.   Amen.

Revelation 4.8. Psalm 71.8. Deuteronomy 32.3. Colossians 1.12.

Blessed are you, O Lord,
Almighty God,
to whom our inmost thoughts are revealed:
you know our needs
much better than we ourselves
can ask or imagine.
Sovereign Lord and ever-loving Redeemer,
in the richness of your mercy
give us pure hearts
to call upon your holy Name;
lead us not into temptation,
but deliver us from evil,
and order all things for our good.

Because all glory, honour and praise
are yours by right,
Father, Son and Holy Spirit,
now and for ever,
to the ages of ages.   Amen.

Luke 6.8. John 13.11. Matthew 6.8,32. Luke 12.30. Ephesians
3.20. 1 Timothy 3.9. 2 Timothy 1.3. Matthew 6.13.

O Lord God,
who in your most holy power
sustain the universe,
be patient with us:
do not be angry at our wicked deeds
but take away our guilt;
remember your compassion and mercy
and in your goodness come to our aid.
In your grace
grant that for what remains of this day
we may be untouched by the scheming of the evil one,
and that we may live our lives in safety,
free from every snare,
through the grace of your Holy Spirit.

Through the grace and mercy
of your only-begotten Son,
to whom with you and your most holy,
gracious and life-giving Spirit
be blessing
now and for ever,
to the ages of ages.   Amen.

Psalm 106.4.

Great and wonderful God,
in your unfathomable goodness and great providence
you have given us the good things of this world,
and furthermore
you have made us a pledge of your eternal kingdom;
during this past day
you have kept us safe from evil:
so grant us to end the day
without sin
in the presence of your divine glory
and to sing hymns to you
who are our God
and who alone are good and loving to everyone.

For you, O God,
are full of mercy
and deep love for mankind:
we give you glory,
Father, Son and Holy Spirit,
now and for ever,
to the ages of ages.   Amen.

Daniel 9.4. Jude 24.

In the evening and the morning and at noon
we praise and bless you,
we pray to you in thanksgiving and supplication.
Father of all,
may our prayer be set before you
like incense
and may our hearts not yield
to the words of the wicked;
deliver us from all
who seek to take possession of our souls.
For our eyes are fixed on you,
O Lord,
our refuge is in you and you are our hope;
do not abandon us, O Lord our God!

For to you belong all glory,
honour and worship,
Father, Son and Holy Spirit,
now and for ever,
to the ages of ages.   Amen.

Psalm 141.2,4,9,8.

Blessed are you, O God, Almighty Lord,
who made the sun to give light to the day
and brightened the night with the shining stars:
you have brought us through this long day
and lead us to the threshold of night;
hear our prayer
and the prayers of your people,
forgive us all
the sins we have committed deliberately or in our
    weakness,
receive our evening supplications,
and pour out upon your inheritors
the riches of your goodness and mercy.
Set your holy angels round about us,
clothe us in the armour of righteousness,
strengthen us with your truth
and defend us with your power;
deliver us from every attack of the devil
who seeks to ensnare us.
Grant that this evening
and the night to come
and all the days of our life
may pass in holiness and peace,
without our falling into sin or error
and untroubled by apparitions and beguiling influences,
through the mediation of the holy Mother of God
and all the saints
who have found favour with you since time began.

For you indeed, O Lord our God,
have mercy on us and save us,
and we glorify you,
Father, Son and Holy Spirit,
now and for ever,
to the ages of ages.   Amen.

Daniel 3.52 (Jerusalem Bible).

O Lord our God,
as you have kept us safe
from the arrow that flies by day,
so preserve us from the pestilence
that stalks in the darkness;
as we lift up our hands to you,
accept this as our evening sacrifice;
as the night proceeds
may we not incur punishment
nor be tempted to do evil;
free us from all anxiety and fear
that might come upon us
through the work of the devil;
let our souls be contrite
and keep our minds concentrated
on the account we are to give you
on the day of your fearful and righteous judgement.
Make our flesh tremble in fear of you,
purify our earth-bound limbs,
that even in the tranquility of sleep
we may rejoice
to gaze on your righteousness;
put far from us all unseemly imagining
and all harmful desires.
Raise us up through this hour of prayer,
and make us strong in faith
to follow the way of your commandments.

Through the great goodness
of your only-begotten Son
who with you and your most holy
and life-giving Spirit
is to be praised
now and for ever,
to the ages of ages.   Amen.

Psalm 91.5–6. Psalm 141.2. Psalm 4.4. Psalm 119.120.
Colossians 3.5.

11

Almighty and eternal God,
in your great love for mankind
you have brought us even at this hour
into the presence of your unfathomable glory
to sing in praise of your wonderful works;
look with favour on us
your unworthy servants,
and grant that with a contrite heart
we may faithfully sing, 'holy, holy, holy, Lord',
and offer you thanksgiving
for the great gifts
that you continually bestow on us.
Remember our weakness, O Lord,
and do not cast us out
on account of our sins:
look with compassion on our wretched condition,
that shunning the darkness of sin
we may walk in the light of righteousness,
and that having put on the armour of light
we may pass our lives
safe from every snare of the enemy,
and so give you the glory in all things,
knowing that you are our Father,
you who are the one true God
abounding in love for all mankind.

For you, Lord, are the holy one,
and we glorify you,
Father, Son and Holy Spirit,
now and for ever
to the ages of ages.   Amen.

Romans 13.12.

O God,
you see and know all things
even before they have their being:
you do not desire the death of sinners
but rather that they may turn to you and live;
so look down from your heavenly dwelling
on your servants these catechumens:
open their ears and hearts
to receive and understand
the mystery of your only-begotten Son
who is our God;
give them new birth
through water and the Spirit
for your eternal kingdom.

That with us
they too may glorify your Name,
which is to be honoured and exalted,
Father, Son and Holy Spirit,
now and for ever,
to the ages of ages.   Amen.

O Lord our God,
we come to you now with open hearts
to call upon your holy Name
and to give you thanks
for keeping us safe during this day
and for bringing us to the light of evening.
We pray that this evening and the approaching night
and all the days of our earthly life
may be free from sin:
clothe us with the armour of your Holy Spirit
to fight against the forces of evil
and the passions of the flesh;
put far from us all sin
and make us worthy of your eternal kingdom.

For to you belong
all glory, honour and praise,
Father, Son and Holy Spirit,
now and for ever
to the ages of ages.   Amen.

Romans 13.12.

O Lord our God,
who live in unapproachable light,
in your great mercy
you have been our constant guide throughout this day
and have called us together
to give you glory at eventide:
hear the prayers
of your unworthy servants
and keeping us safe from the darkness of sin
give light to our souls,
that being ever in awe of you
and going forward in your light
we may glorify you in all things,
who in your unfailing love for all mankind
are the one true God.

For yours is the greatness,
the majesty, the power and the glory,
Father, Son and Holy Spirit,
now and for ever,
to the ages of ages.   Amen.

1 Timothy 6.16.

Great and most high God,
you alone are immortal
and live in unapproachable light;
in your wisdom you created all things,
separating light from darkness,
making the sun to govern the day
and the moon and stars to govern the night.
Though we are sinners
you have allowed us
to come into your presence now
to give you thanks and offer you our evening praise;
in your unfailing love for mankind
let our prayer be set before you
like incense
and accept it as a gentle fragrance.
Grant that this evening and the coming night
may pass in peace:
clothe us in the armour of light,
keep us from fear of the night
and from all that stalks in the darkness,
and may the sleep that you give us
to refresh us in our weakness
be free from troubled dreams.

Creator of the universe and giver of all good things,
may we, stricken in our hearts,
be mindful of your Name,
even as we sleep,
for our inspiration is in meditating
on your commandments;
so let us rejoice with joy in our hearts
and glorify your goodness,
as we bring before you
our prayers and supplications for our sins
and for the sins of your people;
deal mercifully with them
through the mediation of the holy Mother of God.

For you, O God,
are good and loving to everyone
and we give you glory,
Father, Son and Holy Spirit,
now and for ever,
to the ages of ages.   Amen.

1 Timothy 6.16. Psalm 104.2. Psalm 104.24. Genesis 1.14–18.
Psalm 104.19. Psalm 95.2. Psalm 141.2. Exodus 30.7–8. Romans
13.12. Psalm 91.5–6. Psalm 119.143.

O Lord our God,
you parted the heavens
and came down to earth
to save the human race:
look on your inheritance
and on your servants
who bow their heads in meekness before you,
awesome judge,
whose love for all mankind is unbounded.
Your servants do not seek human help:
they count on your mercy
and put their hope in your salvation.
Be their constant protection
this evening and in the coming night
against all assaults and enemies,
against futile thoughts
and false reasoning.

Psalm 18.9. Psalm 144.5. Psalm 94.11.

THAT WE MAY BE DELIVERED FROM THE POWERS OF DARKNESS

Midnight

*About midnight
Paul and Silas were praying
and singing hymns to God.*
Acts 16.25 NIV

O Lord our God,
through your Holy Spirit
you gave us an example in David,
inspiring him to sing psalms
and even at this hour of the night to say:
'At midnight I rise to give you thanks
for your righteous laws';
make us worthy to offer you from the bottom of our
    hearts
our grateful confession of faith;
in your goodness
look with compassion on our wretched state
and at your dreadful day of judgement
let us too be like the faithful and wise servants;
we ask it
through the mediation of the holy Mother of God
and all your saints.

For to you belong
all glory, honour and praise,
Father, Son and Holy Spirit,
now and for ever,
to the ages of ages.   Amen.

Psalm 119.62. Luke 12.42.

Lord,
as we gather here in the middle of the night
we offer you thanksgiving
as far as our strength permits,
and so we pray:
keep safe the treasure of learning
that you set in our hearts,
place on our lips the words of your wisdom
and deliver us from all that lurks in the dark.

For yours is the greatness,
the majesty, the power and the glory,
Father, Son and Holy Spirit,
now and for ever,
to the ages of ages.   Amen.

Psalm 91.6.

Almighty God,
you are Lord of time
and have neither beginning nor end:
you are the redeemer of our souls,
the foundation of human reason
and guardian of our hearts;
through all that you have created
you have revealed your indescribable power;
receive, O Lord,
our supplication
even at this hour of the night,
provide fully for the needs of each one of us
and make us worthy of your goodness.

For your Name
is worthy of all honour and greatness
and is to be glorified with hymns of blessing,
Father, Son and Holy Spirit,
now and for ever,
to the ages of ages.   Amen.

O Lord our God,
in your great goodness
and in the richness of your mercy
you have protected us this night
from the test of evil;
you who are the creator of all things,
bring us safely to the time
when we offer you our prayers at daybreak,
and together with your gift of true light
pour out in our hearts
the treasure of knowing you
that enables us to do your will.

For you, O God,
are good and loving to all mankind
and we give you glory,
Father, Son and Holy Spirit,
now and for ever,
to the ages of ages.   Amen.

O God,
maker of time and creator of all things,
we your helpless servants
bow our heads before you
and so we pray:
send us the blessing of your Spirit
that we may live our lives in all godliness
and in obedience to your commandments.

For you are our God,
the God of salvation and compassion,
and we glorify you,
Father, Son and Holy Spirit,
now and for ever,
to the ages of ages.   Amen.

1 Timothy 2.2.

THAT WE MAY BE TRANSFIGURED BY THE RISING SUN

Dawn

O God, you are my God,
at dawn I seek you.
Psalm 63.1 (Septuagint)

We thank you, O Lord our God,
for making us rise from our beds
and setting upon our lips
these words of praise
so we may worship you and call upon your holy Name.
As you have continually blessed our lives
with goodness and mercy
so we pray to you now: send your help
to those who stand in your holy and glorious presence
awaiting your abundant mercy;
and may those who have served you unceasingly
in love and awe
praise, worship and adore
your unutterable goodness.

For to you belong
all glory, honour and praise,
Father, Son and Holy Spirit,
now and for ever,
to the ages of ages.   Amen.

Psalm 71.8.

Since the darkest hour
our souls have kept their watch before you,
O Lord our God,
for your commandments are light
to the earth.
Teach us to live in holiness and righteousness
and in fear of you
since we glorify you,
the true God.
Hear us, listen to us:
remember, Lord, each one of those
who pray with us here,
and in your power grant them salvation.
Make your people grow in holiness
and bless your inheritance;
give peace to your world
and all your churches,
to those who serve you as priests
and to our rulers and all your people.

For your Name
is worthy of all honour and majesty
and we glorify you in hymns of praise,
Father, Son and Holy Spirit,
now and for ever,
to the ages of ages.   Amen.

Psalm 63.6. Isaiah 26.9. 2 Corinthians 7.1. Psalm 86.1. Psalm
17.6. Psalm 28.9. Psalm 29.11.

Since the darkest hour
our souls have kept their watch before you,
O Lord our God,
for your commandments are light
to the earth.
Teach us, O God,
your righteousness, your precepts and your wisdom.
Enlighten our minds
that we may not slumber in the sin
that leads to death.
Put far from our hearts all darkness,
but give us the sun of your righteousness,
and may the seal of your Holy Spirit
keep us from all harm.
Direct our feet in the way of peace,
let us greet the dawn
and the new day with gladness,
and offer you our morning prayers.

For yours is the greatness,
the majesty, the power and the glory,
Father, Son and Holy Spirit,
now and for ever,
to the ages of ages.   Amen.

Psalm 63.6. Isaiah 26.9. Psalm 119.12,26,135. Ephesians 1.18.
Psalm 119.133. Isaiah 59.8.

Lord God,
you are holy, surpassing human expression:
you made light
shine out of darkness,
and in our night's sleep
you have given us rest:
through you we rise
to give you glory and, prompted by your compassion,
to call upon your goodness;
hear us as we offer you praise
and thanksgiving, as best we are able,
and grant what we ask of you
for our salvation.
Make us children of the light,
inheritors of your eternal goodness;
in the fullness of your mercy, O Lord,
remember all your people:
those who pray with us now
and all our brothers and sisters
across your dominions, on land or sea,
who call on your love for mankind
and beg your help;
extend your great mercy to us all,
that being saved in body and soul
and ever dependent on your love
we may praise your most wonderful
and blessed Name.

For you are the God of compassion,
full of goodness and love for all mankind,
and we give you glory,
Father, Son and Holy Spirit,
now and for ever,
to the ages of ages.   Amen.

2 Corinthians 4.6. 1 Thessalonians 5.5.

Holy Father,
inexhaustible fount of all goodness,
almighty ruler of all,
who perform great wonders,
we worship you and beseech you
in your compassion and holiness
help and uphold us
in our wretched condition.
So remember, O Lord,
those who call upon you:
may our morning prayers
be set before you like incense,
let no one be cast aside
but surround us all with your mercy.
Remember, O Lord,
those who keep watch and sing psalms
to glorify you
together with your only-begotten Son and our God
and your Holy Spirit.
Be their help and deliverance
and receive their supplications
on the spiritual altar of heaven.

For you are our God
and we give you glory,
Father, Son and Holy Spirit,
now and for ever,
to the ages of ages.   Amen.

Psalm 141.2. Psalm 62.7.

We give you thanks,
Lord God of our salvation,
for all that you do
to bless our lives,
so that we may always turn to you,
O saviour and preserver of our souls;
in this past night
you have given us rest
and now you have called us from our beds
to come and adore your holy Name.
And so, O Lord, we pray:
give us grace and strength
to sing to you melodious psalms
and to pray without ceasing
as we await our salvation
in fear and trembling
through the help of your Messiah.
Remember, O Lord,
those who since night-time
have been making their cry to you:
hear them and look with pity on them
and let their unseen enemies
be crushed beneath their feet.

For you are the King of peace
and saviour of our souls,
and we glorify you,
Father, Son and Holy Spirit,
now and for ever,
to the ages of ages.   Amen.

Psalm 68.20. Psalm 47.7. 1 Thessalonians 5.17. Philippians 2.12.
Romans 16.20.

O God and Father of our Lord Jesus Christ,
you have called us from sleep
and brought us together for this hour of prayer,
open our lips
and inspire us with your grace:
accept the thanksgivings
that we lift to you as best we are able
and teach us your will,
for we cannot pray as we should
if you, O Lord, do not guide us
through your Holy Spirit.
And so we pray:
if we have sinned
in thought, word or deed,
whether deliberately or out of weakness,
will you forgive, remit and pardon all our sins,
for if you, Lord, kept a record of our sins,
who could stand?
But with you there is forgiveness and deliverance;
you alone are the holy one, our help,
our refuge and our defence,
and our songs of praise will be always and only yours.

For we celebrate
in hymns of glory and blessing
the power of your majesty,
Father, Son and Holy Spirit,
now and for ever,
to the ages of ages.   Amen.

Psalm 119.12. Romans 8.26. Psalm 130.3,4. Psalm 71.7. Psalm
27.1.

O Lord our God,
you enabled us to cast drowsiness aside
and in calling us to a holy life
you brought us
to lift our hands to you at midnight
to worship you in thanksgiving
for your righteous laws:
so hear now our prayers and supplications:
accept our grateful confession of faith
and our night-time offering of praise.
Give us freely, O God,
a firm faith,
unfailing hope and heartfelt love;
bless us in our going out and coming in,
and in all that we do or say or wish for.
Grant that we may await the break of day
with songs of praise, worship and adoration
as we bless your goodness and indescribable power.

For your most holy Name
is to be celebrated in hymns of blessing
and your majesty is to be glorified,
Father, Son and Holy Spirit,
now and for ever,
to the ages of ages.   Amen.

2 Timothy 1.9. Psalm 134.2. Psalm 119.62. Romans 12.9. Psalm 121.8.

O Lord our God,
through our turning to you
you grant us forgiveness;
you have given us as a pattern
the repentance of David
in order to receive forgiveness,
so that we might acknowledge and confess
our own sinful state;
Lord have mercy on us
according to your great compassion
and in your unfailing love
blot out our sins
and the errors into which we have fallen,
for they are too many to count.
We have sinned against you, O Lord,
against you who know
all the secrets of men's hearts,
and who alone have the power to forgive sins.
When you have created in us a pure heart
and have renewed a steadfast spirit within us,
grant us the joy of your salvation;
do not turn away from us
but in your goodness and gracious favour
and in your love for all mankind
grant that until our dying breath
we may offer you a righteous sacrifice and oblation
at your altars.

Through the grace, compassion
and unceasing love
of your only-begotten Son,
who with you
and your most holy and life-giving Spirit
is to be blessed and glorified
now and for ever,
to the ages of ages.   Amen.

Psalm 51.2,4. Mark 2.10. Psalm 51.10,12,11,19.

O Lord our God,
who have subjected all rational and spiritual powers
to your will,
we pray and beseech you
to accept the praises
we offer you
as best we are able,
together with all creation,
and we ask that you will give us
all the riches of your goodness;
before you every knee shall bow,
in heaven and on earth
and under the earth:
all things living and created
praise your unfathomable glory,
you who are the one true God, abounding in mercy.

With all the powers of heaven
we praise and glorify you,
Father, Son and Holy Spirit,
now and for ever,
to the ages of ages.   Amen.

Philippians 2.10. Psalm 150.6.

Bless too, O Lord,
your servants these catechumens
whom you have brought through a holy calling
to the wonderful light of knowing you:
help them to know
the sure foundation of your word
on which their instruction rests.
Pour your Holy Spirit upon them
that they too may become
the little sheep of the one true shepherd,
signed with the seal of the Holy Spirit
and precious members
of the body of your Church;
and in the world to come
make them worthy
of the real and blessed hope
of the kingdom of heaven.

That with us
they too may glorify your Name
which is worthy of all honour and majesty,
Father, Son and Holy Spirit,
now and for ever,
to the ages of ages.   Amen.

2 Timothy 1.9. John 10.11.

Lord, Lord,
both day and night belong to you,
you formed the light and the sun
and marked the bounds of the earth.
And so we pray:
let your great mercy
shine on our wretchedness
like the dawning light;
free us from darkness
and from the shadow of death,
and from all the attacks and snares
of the evil one.

For we proclaim
the glory and holiness of your Name,
worthy of all honour and majesty,
Father, Son and Holy Spirit,
now and for ever,
to the ages of ages.   Amen.

Luke 1.79.

Lord, Lord,
at your command the day follows its course;
to you all the powers of heaven
address their hymns of praise
and every soul glorifies you,
paying you tribute in worship,
and so we too make our prayer:
grant that we may pass
this day in peace,
that we may be steadfast
and live as is pleasing to you
with a pure heart,
that rejoicing in all your gifts
we may become worthy
ever to celebrate your goodness
in hymns of blessing,
without suffering rebuke.

For to you belong
all glory, honour and praise,
Father, Son and Holy Spirit,
now and for ever,
to the ages of ages.   Amen.

In hymns of praise
we bless and glorify you
and give you thanks,
O God of our fathers,
for you have dispelled the dark cloud of night
and have restored to us the light of day.
In your goodness
forgive our sins,
and in your great mercy
hear our prayer
as we seek refuge in you,
Almighty and most merciful God.
Make the true sun of your righteousness
shine in our hearts,
enlighten our understanding
and protect all our senses,
that walking in confidence
as in the day
in the way of your commandments,
and enjoying your unfathomable light,
we may attain eternal life,
for with you is the fountain of life.

You indeed are the God
of goodness and mercy
and unbounded love
and we glorify you,
Father, Son and Holy Spirit,
now and for ever,
to the ages of ages.   Amen.

2 Corinthians 4.6. Psalm 36.9.

Holy God,
enthroned on high,
and keeping continual watch
over all creation,
we come before you with our heads bowed
and our hearts humbled,
and so we pray:
stretch out your unseen hand
from your holy dwelling place
to bless us all,
and if we have sinned in any way,
whether deliberately or in weakness,
forgive us,
O God of goodness and infinite love,
who bestow on us all the good things of this earth.

You, indeed, O God,
are pleased to have compassion on us and save us,
and we glorify you,
Father, Son and Holy Spirit,
now and for ever,
to the ages of ages.   Amen.

Psalm 113.5. Psalm 33.14.

Most holy God,
we pray and beseech you,
give each of us a pure heart
and a way of speaking
that befits the faith we profess;
grant us uprightness of purpose,
powers of reasoning unhindered by passions,
conduct that becomes those who fear you,
and perfect knowledge of your commandments;
may we enjoy health
in body and in spirit.
Grant us a life of peace,
genuine faith and living hope,
sincere charity and bountiful generosity,
patience that knows no bounds
and the light of your truth
to proclaim your goodness to us,
that for ever and in all things
placing our trust only in you
we may abound in every good work,
and that in Christ
your gifts may increase
in every soul.

For to you belong
all glory, honour and majesty,
Father, Son and Holy Spirit,
now and for ever,
to the ages of ages.   Amen.

Psalm 51.10.

Hear us, O Lord our God,
and have pity on us
for you are merciful.
May our steps hold to your paths,
and may our feet not slip:
guide us, Lord, in your way
and we shall walk in your truth.
May our prayer come before you, O Lord:
turn your ear to our cry
for our souls are full of trouble
and our life draws near the grave.
Remember us, O Lord,
in your goodness
and visit us with your salvation!

For you are the God of all mercy
and full of compassion,
yours is the glory,
Father, Son and Holy Spirit,
now and for ever,
to the ages of ages.   Amen.

Psalm 17.5. Psalm 86.11. Psalm 88.2,3. Psalm 106.4.

THAT WE MAY RECEIVE THE HOLY SPIRIT IN HIS FULLNESS

9.00 a.m.

*All of them were filled
with the Holy Spirit
and began to speak
in other tongues . . .
[it was] only nine
in the morning.*

Acts 2.4,15 NIV

O God,
you have graciously brought us
to this hour,
the time when you poured out
your Holy Spirit
in tongues of fire
upon your apostles,
filling them with the gift
of your grace;
so, most wonderful Lord,
may we too receive this blessing;
and as we seek to praise you,
merciful God,
in psalms and hymns and spiritual songs,
may we share in your eternal kingdom.

For your Name
is worthy of all honour and majesty
and you are to be glorified in hymns of blessing,
Father, Son and Holy Spirit,
now and for ever,
to the ages of ages.   Amen.

Acts 2.1–4. Ephesians 5.19. Colossians 3.16.

O Lord our God,
at the third hour
you poured out the grace of your Holy Spirit
upon your holy and glorious apostles:
so purify our minds,
and let them be without stain or blemish,
that approaching your fearful Name
with cleansed hearts
we may enjoy
the good things promised to us.

Through the mercy of your Christ
with whom and the most holy and life-giving Spirit
you are to be worshipped
now and for ever
to the ages of ages.   Amen.

Acts 2.1–4. Ephesians 5.27.

O God,
you cre   osts
to glor
and y   men,
withi
to of   vn behalf
pra   n and supplication
for   committed,
ar   ks for the good things
w   vard us:
                 s
               now,
             we call upon you
that we   ave salvation.

For yours is the greatness,
the power and the glory,
Father, Son and Holy Spirit,
now and for ever,
to the ages of ages.   Amen.

O Lord
you have honoured us with your own image
and given us free will,
so deliver us from all afflictions that oppress us;
keep us in faith and righteousness
all the days of our life
and let us do all things
in accordance with your will.

For yours is the greatness,
the majesty, the power and the glory,
Father, Son and Holy Spirit,
now and for ever,
to the ages of ages.   Amen.

Genesis 1.27.

Hear our prayer, O Lord:
bless, protect and sanctify
all those who bow their heads
before you.

Through the grace,
mercy and infinite love
of your only-begotten Son,
to whom with you and your most holy,
gracious and life-giving Spirit
be blessing
now and for ever,
to the ages of ages.   Amen.

Psalm 86.6. Numbers 6.24.

THAT WE MAY
ACKNOWLEDGE GOD'S
PRESENCE DAILY

Noon

About noon . . .
Peter went up on the roof
to pray.
Acts 10.9 NIV

O Lord, our God and King,
this was the hour
you stretched out your undefiled hands
on the cross which we adore,
cancelling the record of our sins,
and nailing it to the cross:
remit now
every debt of sin
and set us free from the condemnation
which our evil thoughts, words or deeds deserve,
so that with pure hearts
we may at all times offer you
the worship that is your due.

For to you belong
all glory, honour and praise,
Father, Son and Holy Spirit,
now and for ever,
to the ages of ages.   Amen.

Colossians 2.14.

O Lord our God,
in Peter,
the foremost of the apostles,
you have given us an example
of prayer at midday:
turn to us,
your helpless and unworthy servants,
preserve us from misfortune
and from the plague that destroys at midday,
deliver us, O God,
from all evil
for the rest of this day.

For yours is the greatness,
the power and the glory,
Father, Son and Holy Spirit,
now and for ever,
to the ages of ages.   Amen.

Acts 10.9. Psalm 91.6.

O Lord, our King and our God,
heaven is your throne
and earth your footstool,
you set bounds to the universe
while knowing yourself no limitation:
do not look with anger on your servants,
keep us safe and protect us
from the deceitful vanities of this world,
whether words or deeds,
and guide us according to your will.

For we celebrate
your holy and glorious Name,
worthy of all honour and praise,
Father, Son and Holy Spirit,
now and for ever,
to the ages of ages.   Amen.

Isaiah 66.1.

Eternal God,
you live in impenetrable light:
no one has ever seen you
nor is able to see you,
who are the everlasting source of eternal blessing;
it is you, Lord of creation,
who protect us
who have put our hope in you,
being filled with your wondrous
divine grace.

For yours is the greatness,
the majesty, the power and the glory,
Father, Son and Holy Spirit,
now and for ever,
to the ages of ages.   Amen.

O Lord our God,
look down from your holy and lofty dwelling
on all who live on earth,
and keep in peace and well-being
all those
who bow their heads
beneath your Messiah's yoke.

For your Name,
worthy of all honour and majesty,
is to be praised
in hymns of blessing and glory,
Father, Son and Holy Spirit,
now and for ever,
to the ages of ages.   Amen.

Psalm 33.14.

THAT WE MAY BE STRONG
AT THE TIME OF TRIAL

3.00 p.m.

One day Peter and John
were going up to the temple
at the time of prayer –
at three in the afternoon.
Acts 3.1 NIV

Sovereign Lord,
God of all power and glory,
you heard your holy apostles Peter and John
when they went to pray
at the ninth hour,
and so enabled them
to perform a miracle of healing
in front of all the people:
give us a sign of your goodness
that we may count as nothing the weapons of the enemy
and may regard his temptations
as having no more strength than a child.

For yours is the greatness,
the power and the glory,
Father, Son and Holy Spirit,
now and for ever,
to the ages of ages.   Amen.

Acts 3.1. Psalm 86.17.

O Lord our God,
you did not reject mankind
when he fell into sin,
but through your plan of salvation
and your holy mysteries
you made us fit for the kingdom of heaven:
you are the all-loving King,
so be to us who call upon you
our shield and our defence
against every danger that awaits us
from the snares of the enemy;
restore instead our hope in you,
our deliverer and our redeemer.

For we praise your holy and glorious Name,
that is worthy of all honour and majesty,
Father, Son and Holy Spirit,
now and for ever,
to the ages of ages.   Amen.

O Lord,
when we consider what we are
and remember our mistakes,
then, conscious of our sins and misdeeds,
our thoughts turn
to your terrible day of judgement;
our assurance of a favourable verdict
lies in our one and only refuge
who loves all mankind;
and so it is right
that we pray you now
to grant us
the great gift of your merciful forbearance.

Through the grace, mercy
and all-embracing love
of your only-begotten Son,
to whom with you
and your holy and life-giving Spirit
be all blessing,
now and for ever,
to the ages of ages.   Amen.

O God,
it is your will
that we should pray continually
without ever becoming weary
so that our adversary the devil may not find a way
of attacking our souls:
protect us from this generation
and make us fit
to enter the number of those
who will be at your right hand
on the day of your righteous judgement.

For to you
belong all glory, honour and praise,
Father, Son and Holy Spirit,
now and for ever,
to the ages of ages.   Amen.

Luke 18.1.

Hear us, O Lord,
and answer us:
bless and sanctify
all those
whose heads are bowed
in your presence
and make them worthy
of your all-embracing love.

You indeed, O God,
are our saviour
and your majesty is eternal,
Father, Son and Holy Spirit,
now and for ever,
to the ages of ages.   Amen.

Psalm 86.1.

THAT WE MAY FOLLOW THE LORD IN ALL HIS WAYS

Afternoon

Evening, morning and noon
I cry out in distress
and he hears my voice.
Psalm 55.17 NIV

O Lord,
you sit enthroned between the cherubim
and the seraphim give you glory:
look down on us,
your wretched and unworthy servants,
and stir our hearts
to celebrate your wonderful goodness.
Keep us from all snares of the enemy,
that, bathed in your light
and guided by your will to do good,
we may become worthy of your heavenly kingdom
and be counted among
the number of your chosen ones.

For you are our God,
the God of mercy and salvation,
and we glorify you,
Father, Son and Holy Spirit,
now and for ever,
to the ages of ages.   Amen.

Psalm 80.1.

We beseech you, O Lord our God,
be patient with us sinners.
You who know our weakness,
protect the work of your hands
now and in times to come,
deliver us from all temptation
and all danger
and from the powers of darkness of this world,
and bring us
into the kingdom of your only Son and our God.

For to your most holy Name
be the glory,
Father, Son and Holy Spirit,
now and for ever,
to the ages of ages.   Amen.

Psalm 138.8. Colossians 1.13.

Almighty Lord God,
your glory cannot be approached,
your compassion knows no bounds,
and your love for all mankind
is beyond human expression;
in your mercy
look on us
and all your people:
do not leave us to our sins
but deal with us according to your goodness.
Guide us to the haven of your will
and make us truly obedient
to your commandments,
that we may not feel ashamed
when we come before your Messiah's dread judgement
    seat.

For you, O God,
are good and ever-loving,
and we glorify you,
Father, Son and Holy Spirit,
now and for ever,
to the ages of ages.   Amen.

Lord God of our fathers,
you enable those who ask
to pray,
and you receive your servants' supplications
as they cry to you night and day:
so incline your ear
and hear the prayer of us sinners.
You know our inner nature
and our weakness:
do not remember our past sins
but remember rather, O Lord,
that we are dust,
a breath of air that passes and is lost;
in your compassion
keep our lives in the shelter of your mighty arm.
Guide us along the right path
to follow the way
of your commandments,
teach us to do your will,
to speak as you would have us do
and to meditate day and night on your law.
Command your holy angels
to guard us in all our ways,
to deliver us from the arrow that flies by day
and whatever stalks in the darkness,
from the plague and from the demon
that roves at midday.
Let your praise be on our tongues
and joy on our lips,
that through grace we may sing
psalms and hymns and spiritual songs,
and may our hearts be filled
with the music of your praise
as we offer you thanksgiving,
O God of all creation
and saviour of all who trust
in the richness of your mercy.

For you, O God,
are good and loving to all mankind,
and we glorify you,
Father, Son and Holy Spirit,
now and for ever,
to the ages of ages.   Amen.

Psalm 86.1. Psalm 91.11,5,6. Psalm 71.8. Psalm 63.5.

Almighty God,
in your love for all mankind
look down from your heavenly dwelling
on these catechumens, your servants,
who have their heads bowed
in your presence
and await your compassion:
reveal to them
your Gospel of righteousness,
count them among your chosen flock
and in your good time
grant them new birth
from the waters of baptism.

That they too, with us,
may glorify your Name,
Father, Son and Holy Spirit,
now and for ever,
to the ages of ages.   Amen.

O Lord our God,
look mercifully on us
and on those who are preparing
for Holy Baptism,
and have their heads bowed before you now:
make the light of your Gospel
shine upon them;
send an angel of light
to deliver them from all powers of the enemy,
that when they are fit to receive your immortal gift
and are brought into a life
of obedience to your commandments,
they may know the joys of heaven.

For you are their light
and we glorify you,
Father, Son and Holy Spirit,
now and for ever,
to the ages of ages.   Amen.

O Lord our God,
at your coming
you set men free
from the worship of other gods:
by your miracles
you taught us to acknowledge you
as the one creator and only maker
of all things living,
and to place our hope in you:
protect us by the power of your Name,
sanctify us by your truth
and pour out your mercy upon us
and upon all your people.

For you are our God,
the God of mercy and salvation,
and we glorify you,
Father, Son and Holy Spirit,
now and for ever,
to the ages of ages.   Amen.

John 17.11,17.

O Lord our God,
you reduced our human lifetime to a little while,
because of our weak and defenceless nature:
but in return,
if we overcome the assaults of the enemy,
you have promised us eternal joy.
Strengthen us, Father,
as we stand in fear of you,
give us power in your words
and guide us in your righteousness.

For you are God,
the God of mercy and salvation,
and we glorify you,
Father, Son and Holy Spirit,
now and for ever,
to the ages of ages.   Amen.

O Lord our God,
you alone are good
and full of love for all mankind;
you alone are righteous and just,
you alone are long-suffering and merciful;
you are our God
and Father of our Lord Jesus Christ,
who was crucified under Pontius Pilate,
rose again on the third day
and entered into his glory
which is your glory;
so we pray:
give grace to us your servants
and strengthen us with your Gospel of righteousness.
Father of mercy,
may your will
bring light to every part of our being
and cleanse us from all malice and sin;
keep us pure and blameless
whenever the devil may interfere,
and in your goodness, Lord,
grant that we may learn more of you
and come to a better understanding of your nature,
that we might stand in awe of you
and do what is pleasing to you
until the end of our days,
until our final hour
and our dying breath.
Father,
we sinners acclaim you our true God,
that in your unutterable goodness
you may set your seal
upon our hearts and souls
and on our spirits,
and will defend them from wicked demons,
poisonous snakes
and wild animals,

from evil and slander,
depravity and vanity,
fornication and greed,
disease and weakness,
falsehood and conspiracy
and from all the snares of our enemy.
Incorruptible Father,
surround your servants with your mercy,
do not forsake us,
and let us not be the cause
of our enemies' wicked rejoicing,
nor of the people's scorn,
nor of respite for the forces of evil;
but let your goodness and mercy
accompany us
all the days of our life.

For yours is the greatness,
the majesty, the power and the glory,
Father, Son and Holy Spirit,
now and for ever,
to the ages of ages.   Amen.

Psalm 23.

O Lord our God,
from your throne of glory
you look down in your compassion
through the heights that divide us
to watch over our wretched condition:
bless us all
who bow down in your presence
and in your goodness raise us up.

With hymns of blessing and glory
may your holy and merciful Name
be praised,
Father, Son and Holy Spirit,
now and for ever,
to the ages of ages.   Amen.

Daniel 3.54,53 (Jerusalem Bible).

GIVE GLORY TO GOD WHO DOES MARVELLOUS THINGS

Night-time

You . . . who minister by night in the house of the Lord.
Lift up your hands in the sanctuary
and praise the Lord.

Psalm 134.1–2 NIV

O Lord,
we have rejoiced greatly by day
at the sight of the magnificent works
revealed in your creation;
and being filled with wonder,
we have glorified you
as the creator of the universe
who have done marvellous things;
so now,
as we come to the end of this day,
it is fitting
that we offer you our praise.
And we remember
your wisdom and omniscience,
for you have brought the darkness
and it has become night,
giving men rest from their labours
and giving animals a time to seek food;
for this,
we proclaim aloud the words of the psalmist:
'How many are your works, O Lord!
In wisdom you made them all'.
Moreover we beg you,
ever-loving Father,
Sun of righteousness,
do not turn away from us
in annoyance at our sins,
but surround us always
with the light of your grace,
that day and night
we may glorify your immeasurable greatness.

For to you belong
all glory, honour and praise,
Father, Son and Holy Spirit,
now and for ever,
to the ages of ages.   Amen.

Psalm 104.20,21,24.

O Lord our God,
you are the eternal light
that never grows dim:
in you there is no change
nor hint of any decline;
now at this evening hour we sing to you
and ask that we may remain awake,
that our eyes may stay open,
and grant that the thoughts of our hearts
may turn to the contemplation of your glory.
May our souls, we pray,
not fall victim to sleep,
so depriving us of that spiritual voice
that rejoices in you
and gives you praise and thanksgiving;
rather,
as we sing to you, O God,
with our lips and in our hearts
psalms, hymns and spiritual songs,
may we attain the salvation that comes from you,
that we may rejoice for ever
in the praises at your heavenly banquet.

For we celebrate your holy and glorious Name,
which is worthy of all honour and majesty,
Father, Son and Holy Spirit,
now and for ever,
to the ages of ages.   Amen.

Ephesians 5.19. Colossians 3.16.

O God,
without ever growing weary
you accept the praise
of the incorporeal powers of heaven,
who have no need of physical light,
having been given
the eternal brightness
of your impenetrable glory:
with your consent
they celebrate your holiness
in unending worship.
Look upon our misery
and receive the night-time praises
that we offer you,
following the example of the heavenly host,
in so far as our human weakness allows us.
Do not look on the unworthiness of our lives:
in your unbounded goodness
you created us from nothing
and sustain our being.
Through your holy scriptures
you have inspired in us
the fragrance of your praise
and the duty of praising you,
who alone are holy,
immeasurable and beyond human expression,
creator and Lord of all things.
On our knees we glorify you,
beseeching you to set us free
from the darkness of sin,
and to bless us eternally
with the light of your countenance.

For yours is the greatness,
the majesty, the power and the glory,
Father, Son and Holy Spirit,
now and for ever,
to the ages of ages.   Amen.

Sovereign Lord,
incomprehensible in being
and source of unattainable light,
Father of the only-begotten Word
who is one substance with you,
from you proceeds
the all-powerful Spirit,
the fount of life.
You did not keep mankind
imprisoned in the darkness of sin,
but through the Law and the Prophets
you made the divine light of your holy Word
shine upon us,
and in another age
you were pleased to let your only Son,
the real and incomprehensible Sun of righteousness,
become flesh for our sake,
to lead us towards the splendour of your light.
May your ears be attentive
to our prayer:
we await the day of your Messiah, our God,
the judge of all;
so grant that we may pass this night
with a watchful and sober spirit,
that we may not become drowsy and fall asleep
but be wakeful and alert
to obey your commandments;
that we may enter into the joy of that same Lord,
where there is no more pain or suffering or sorrow,
the dwelling-place of all who delight in you.

For you, O God,
are good and ever-loving
and we glorify you,
Father, Son and Holy Spirit,
now and for ever,
to the ages of ages.   Amen.

Psalm 130.2. Revelation 21.4.

O Lord our God,
make our hearts
obedient to your divine will;
turn our eyes
away from vain things,
that, free from the world's attractions,
they may always look
on your glorious beauty.

For you are our God,
the God of compassion and salvation,
and we glorify you,
Father, Son and Holy Spirit,
now and for ever,
to the ages of ages.   Amen.

The Liturgy of the Hours of the 'Great Church':
Themes of the Euchologion and Liturgical Structures

*This study is reproduced with some modifications and without
critical apparatus; readers needing this are advised to consult the
original Italian edition:* Il Signore della Gloria *(Edizione Paoline,
Milan 1988).*

The liturgical unit or *rite* which is commonly known as
Byzantine, is, nowadays at least, far from being a unified
whole. Just as today's Roman rite combines the liturgical
tradition of Rome with foreign cultic and cultural idioms, so
the 'Byzantine' rite in its present form is the result of a more
or less spontaneous merging of the authentic *Byzantine*
rite (that of the cathedral of Constantinople, the 'Great
Church') with the rites of the cathedral at Jerusalem and the
monasteries of Palestine.

1. *Formative period*

In 315 Constantine the Great decided to transfer the capital
of his empire to the banks of the Bosphorus and this became
the centre of the *oikoumene* or 'civilised world'. The place he
chose, Old Byzantium, was in ecclesiastical terms only a
suffragan see of the metropolitan cathedral of Heraclea. It
was not as yet designated 'apostolic'; that title was claimed
later in order to justify the *presbeia tes times*, or 'primacy of
honour', granted to it in canon III of the Council of Constantinople (381) and in canon XXVIII of the Council of
Chalcedon (451). This move was primarily political and apart
from giving the emperor's city the new function of directing
the church, its effect was limited to providing a suitable
canonical instrument for the formal recognition of jurisdic-
tion already exercised *de facto* over the 'dioceses' of Thrace,
Asia and Pontus.

The organisation of the church and liturgy of the New
Rome thus fell to the ecumenical Councils of Constantinople
(381), and Ephesus (431). This is a crucial period in the
history of liturgy, following the appearance of the first
written formularies. Various local rites, like their ecclesi-

astical areas, began to take shape at a few principal sees (later called *patriarchates*); their identity was expressed through the *language* of their ritual and this was the result not of a synthesis of different existing indigenous traditions, but of a gradual process of coming together with occasional deliberate adjustments.

Byzantium was much influenced in this respect by Antioch, that theological and liturgical laboratory of ancient Christendom, and helped by the contributions of various Antiochene bishops, most notably John Chrysostom (398–404) and Nestorius (428–451). To understand the mutual dependence of these two centres, one need only compare various Byzantine *euchologia* with similar ones in the *Apostolic Constitutions*, a Greek work compiled around 380 by a Syrian living near Antioch; it would, however, be a mistake to interpret this dependence too narrowly, since it is more likely that a common source has influenced both texts.

There is a further typically 4th-century phenomenon, belonging as much to the Old as to the New Rome, that had a great influence on the structure of liturgies, especially eucharistic ones. This is contemporary Christianity's intense interest in the Holy Places and 'memorials' of apostles and martyrs. Pilgrims were coming into contact with a liturgy where the *day*, *time* and *place* were of the first importance and this resulted in attempts to reproduce *to scale* in their own cities the toponymy of Jerusalem and Palestine, which in turn gave rise to a liturgy of the *stations* type. The basilicas in Rome dedicated to the Mother of God and to the Cross were given the names of 'S. Maria Maggiore' – 'at the manger' – (= Bethlehem) and of 'S. Croce in *Jerusalem*', while at Constantinople the various sanctuaries built to house famous relics became the focal points of the stations liturgy. It follows, therefore, that the Eucharist was not celebrated *every* day in *all* the city churches, but only in churches chosen *ad hoc* because they had some particular link with the day in question. Clergy and people would come in procession – *lite* – and in Rome such churches became known as *stations*.

The reason for these topographic foundations of liturgy is not to be sought in purely sentimental or devotional needs; it is something which should be seen instead as a product of the developing theology of the time. Christianity became a state religion at the very moment when the cult was ceasing to be a pure and simple expression of a synthesised eschatological faith (with Easter being the one and only festival); instead it was becoming a means of *sustaining* the faith of the huge numbers of newly baptised Christians. So the liturgy acquired a descriptive, mystical dimension: it portrayed and gave emphasis to specific episodes in the life of Christ and his Mother, and lost its single vision, its single celebration, of Christ's act of redemption. In short, the cult became historicising.

2. *The first written text: the euchologion Barberini gr 336*

The manuscript which the distinguished French liturgist J. Goar called the 'Barberinum Scti Marci' is a small parchment Codex. Its content is what is defined as a *Euchologion* – a simple collection of prayers for use by the celebrant (priest or bishop). These are divided according to 'argument', generally in numbered sequence, and preceded by brief rubrics which are usually no more than the title of the prayer. In places various diaconal litanies are inserted between the prayers of each rite or grouped together at the end of the manuscript; such litanies are usually collected in a separate booklet called a *diakonikon*. It is however reasonable to suppose that the Barberini scribe was making a synthesis from several sources available to him. At ff 266–279 there are extracts from the *Apostolic Constitutions* which were originally placed at the beginning of the Codex.

The great importance of the Barberini lies in the fact that it is still the oldest surviving Byzantine *Euchologion*. Its existence has been attested since the 8th Century and the manuscript does provide evidence for a reliable dating; the earliest text is one of the 'ambo' prayers attributed to the patriarch Germanus I (715–730), and the latest is a Latin prayer at the end of the Codex which can be no later than the first years of the 9th Century, at the outside. This means that the Barberini gives us a form of the Byzantine rite that predates the age of iconoclasm with its devastating effect on the formation of the Constantinople liturgy.

The question of origin is more problematic. Past authors especially have suggested a Constantinople source, others a Palestinian one, and yet others have favoured an Italian origin. This third hypothesis is certainly the most likely, since the structure of the Liturgy (i.e. the eucharistic formulary) attributed to St John Chrysostom reveals a basic structure and euchological content which are typical of southern Italy. The presence of 'patriarchal' rites belonging to the liturgy of the Capital, such as the Emperor's coronation, or the catechism recited by baptism candidates on the morning of Good Friday, is explained by the fact that the Barberini's compiler must have had one or more sources from that tradition in front of him. Our illustrious manuscript might therefore be defined as a *euchologion* copied in southern Italy (perhaps Calabria) from a Constantinople original, with various local adaptations and some Palestinian elements.

Over the centuries the Codex has changed hands several times. It belonged to the acquisitive Florentine humanist Niccolo Niccoli (1363–1437) and was subsequently owned by the preaching order of the monks of St Mark, also in Florence. It eventually ended up in the Vatican Library, via the noble Barberini family of Rome, and is still there in the archives named after them.

3. *Space as liturgical expression: the cathedral of Hagia Sophia*

In no liturgical tradition was liturgical space as integral a part of the liturgy as in the Byzantine one and in no tradition did a building play such a decisive role as Justinian's *Hagia Sophia*. The cathedral had been built on the ruins of Constantine's basilica which was destroyed in the Nika riot of January 532; it was reconsecrated by Patriarch Menas on 27 December 537 in the presence of Justinian himself who is said to have exclaimed:

> Glory and praise to the most high God
> who has allowed me in my unworthiness
> to complete such a work!
> Solomon I have surpassed you!

The emperor's pride is echoed in an enthusiastic description by the historian Procopius of Caesarea in his *De aedificiis*:

> . . . Columns rise up from the floor . . . positioned like a choir to support that part of the building which is constructed in a crescent shape . . . When you go in to pray you realise at once that this is not a creation of human skill or talent but of God, and as the mind turns to God it already moves in heaven, knowing that he is not far off but

is in a very special way enjoying this seat that he himself has chosen.

Procopius is here anticipating the idea of a church as heaven on earth, which was later developed by Maximus the Confessor; for him the church building was a spatial icon, a symbol of the eschatological church and at the same time (as Justinian, at least, intended it) the Temple *par excellence* of the New Covenant, rivalling the temple at Jerusalem. There was only one difference between the two buildings: the ancient temple was unique and inimitable, but Hagia Sophia, by contrast, was to be the model for all the other churches in the city and all the cathedrals in the Empire. It was seen as the privileged place of worship, a 'cathedral' that by its very nature is a model, where the very *qahal Jahwe* of the Old Testament is reinterpreted by the redeemed messianic community as the prime expression of its self-consciousness; thus each local church in particular, as organised and represented by its ministers, becomes the symbol, or icon, of the whole Church of God.

Hagia Sophia is also the supreme example of a genuinely liturgical building, where there is little that is merely decorative. Each space was conceived as relating to a specific point in worship and was regulated by a clearly defined architectural mystagogy. Thus the narthex was the place for the long antiphonal psalmody of *Orthros* and *Lychnikon*; these were the cardinal points of the daily liturgy of the Hours; after that the service of praise was focused on the majestic ambo that dominated the vast central nave: this was the place reserved for the priestly mediator once the litanies and priest's prayers had been said in the sanctuary or presbytery.

Justinian built other churches, such as Hag. Eirene, Hag. Sergios and Bacchos and Mother-of-God of Blachernes, but Hagia Sophia remains without parallel, the epitome of the architectural conception of that great work of art, the attempt to construct a Christian Roman Empire.

4. *Sources of the Liturgy of the Hours of the 'Great Church'*

Between its formative period in the 4th Century, when the Byzantine rite took on its distinctive appearance, and the first *euchologion* in the 8th Century, there are only a few fragmentary references to the Constantinople Liturgy of the Hours, and these are often no more than vague allusions.

Gregory of Nazianzus, called 'the theologian' (died *c.* 390), refers in his famous *Farewell Discourse* to the *staseis pannychoi* or pauses (stations) throughout the night. This is echoed by the historian Sozomen who, in his *Church History* (439–450) writes of people singing 'hymns in the morning and at night'. John Chrysostom for his part seems in various places to recommend vigils in honour of martyrs, and he was himself to institute festal vigils, in opposition to those already practised by the Arians, and night-time processions (*nychterinai litaneiai*). These were looked on with disfavour by the capital's lazy clergy, who were subsequently ordered, under Justinian's Codex of 528, to celebrate the morning, evening and night-time offices in public. The tradition of the cathedral vigil (not to be confused with the *agrypnia* or *all-night vigil* still practised today, for example in the Russian Church) was maintained in Constantinople at least until the end of the iconoclastic persecutions.

As for the *euchologion* period, the extant sources can be subdivided into four distinct types: 1) lists of *euchologia* spanning the 8th to the 14th Centuries; 2) books of rubrics regulating the conduct of the year's liturgical events; 3) the *antiphonaria* with the Psalter subdivided into sixty-eight antiphons, each containing one or more psalms, arranged in a fortnightly cycle; this is sometimes attributed to the Patriarch Anthimus who was deposed in 536; 4) documents of a descriptive or catechetical nature, like the travel diary of Archbishop Antony of Novgorod who visited Constantinople around 1200, and the writings of the great prelate and liturgist Simeon of Thessalonica (d. 1429); Simeon, however, is describing a liturgy of the Hours that had already become monasticised and was undoubtedly dying out.

5. *The structure of the daily 'cursus' and special occasions*

The ancient 'cathedral' Liturgy of the Hours of Hagia Sophia is described as *asmatike akolouthia* (= a sung service) or, more simply, as *asmatikos*, an expression coined by Simeon of Thessalonica to distinguish it from monastic daily prayer of a more meditative nature that was recited rather than sung.

This liturgy, common to all the *Catholic* churches (*katholikon* = cathedral) of the *oikoumene* (= Empire), was celebrated regularly in Hagia Sophia until the early 13th Century when it gradually fell into disuse. In Simeon's opinion this was because of the Frankish capture of Constantinople during the fourth crusade (1204). This, together with the creation of a Latin patriarch, made its use impossible since, among other things, it demanded a large number of clerics and singers. The *asmatikos* was thus limited to occasional celebrations, although it survived for a long time in the cathedral of Hagia Sophia at Thessalonica, until that city was occupied by the Turks on 29 March 1430, six months after Simeon's death.

The daily 'cursus' of the *asmatike akolouthia* normally comprised six acts of worship: *Lychnikon* or *Hesperinos*, *Mesonyktikon*, *Orthros* and the Hours of *Terce*, *Sext* and *None*. *Lychnikon* (sunset) or *Hesperinos* (vespers) is solemn prayer at sunset, something that is common to all liturgical traditions. Here the Church gives thanks to God for the gift of physical light and gazes on Christ, the perpetual sun shining on the universe; the work of the past day is offered to God, his pardon is sought for sins committed and intercession is made for all mankind. *Mesonyktikon* (the midnight office) was a night-time service which could take place at any time between 9.00 p.m. and 3.00 a.m., and was perhaps more relevant to the monastic communities who were attached to Hagia Sophia when there was no cathedral congregation. *Orthros* (dawn) is the morning equivalent of *Lychnikon*, analogous to *Lauds* in the Roman rite. The new day is dedicated to God in praise and in thanksgiving to Christ, the Sun of righteousness, who by his resurrection has freed us from the powers of darkness. *Terce*, *Sext* and *None* are pauses for prayer during the day when Christians, following the apostles' example and in obedience to the Lord's command, commemorate the paschal mysteries (Christ's crucifixion and death at the sixth and ninth hours, and the pouring out of the Spirit at Pentecost at the third hour) and seek absolution from Him who knows neither rest nor tiredness.

From the 11th Century onwards *Prime* is also included in the *euchologia*, but the prayers are often incomplete or supplemented by ones from the other Hours. This can only be seen as an innovation that is neither felicitous nor appropriate.

On some occasions, and at times when the liturgy was flourishing, other offices like *Pannychis* and *Tritoekte* were incorporated into the ordinary *cursus*.

Contrary to what is implied by its etymology, *Pannychis* (= all-night) was a festal vigil associated with the major feasts and with Lent; it was added on to the *Lychnikon* and ended with the singing of the *kontakion*, the most famous of which is the *Akathistos* to the Mother of God. Late in the evening of Good Friday there was the *Pannychis* of 'the passion of our Lord Jesus Christ' involving the reading of twelve passages from the Gospels relating to the Passion. The *Pannychis* was probably also used as a vigil for the dead and thus as a genuine funeral office, but there is no mention of this in the ancient *euchologia*, where there are simply series of prayers under different headings.

Unlike *Pannychis*, *Tritoekte* (= between the third and sixth hours), which was the late morning office took place on the ferial days in Lent that were non-liturgical (i.e. without a Eucharist). The morning of Good Friday was especially important: the patriarch presided and candidates for baptism would renounce Satan and make their profession of faith.

From a structural point of view each individual celebration of the *asmatike akolouthia* was composed of five elements: psalms, prayers, litanies, sometimes hymns, and biblical readings.

The psalms, which are a characteristic feature of the Liturgy of the Hours in all traditions, were arranged in fixed and variable antiphons, so as to form a liturgical unit which was made up of one or more psalms and always ended with the doxology. After a certain number of verses the congregation would join in singing refrains that were short and easy to remember. The antiphons formed the introductory part of each service; there were eight of them for *Lychnikon* and *Orthros* (reduced to three on Sundays and feast days) and three for the other Hours.

Each antiphon was preceded by a prayer spoken by the president that might be called 'psalmic': – the psalm could be paraphrased or interpreted in the light of the New Testament (as with some of the prayers preceding set antiphons and Psalms 50 and 148–150 at *Orthros*), or introduced in a general way without specific reference to the text.

After the antiphons had been sung in the narthex at *Lychnikon*, *Orthros* and *Tritoekte* the celebrants and congregation entered the nave, where the most characteristic part of each Hour took place: *Prokeimenon*, the 'Kyrie eleison' litany and three 'little antiphons' at *Lychnikon*; Psalm 50 with *troparion*, the 'praise' psalms (148–150), 'Gloria in excelsis', *Prokeimenon* and Gospel readings at *Orthros*; and *troparion*, readings from the Prophets and the 'Kyrie eleison' litany at *Tritoekte*. With the exception of the final Hour, which allowed for a special litany and prayers for baptism candidates and, like *Orthros* and *Lychnikon*, a prayer and a litany for catechumens, all the Hours ended with two litanies and prayers of the faithful; then there was a third litany, that of the *Angel of peace*, followed by a so-called prayer of *apolysis* (= dismissal) and a final solemn prayer of blessing over the faithful as they bowed their heads (= *kephaloklisia*). The rite ended with the deacon's charge: 'Let us go out in peace.'

At *Lychnikon* there was provision for Bible readings after the antiphons on the vigils of the Nativity and Epiphany, and during the Easter vigil at the end of that same evening service, in order to lead into *Pannychis*; similarly at the end of *Orthros*, either as a 'divine reading' or as a right and proper catechism for baptism candidates.

6. *Euchological themes*

'Separating the light from the darkness God himself was the first to celebrate the *Lychnikon* and *Orthros* of creation: And there was evening and there was morning – the first day (Genesis 1.5).' Evening prayers and morning supplications are a constant and universal phenomenon in all religions; we have examples of this from Ancient Israel in the Temple worship and from Judaism in the prayers at the synagogue and at home.

In the president's prayers in the *asmatikos*, worshipping God's glory is above all an act of thanksgiving to God who himself takes the initiative in calling us to prayer. It is not an act of personal choice or the fulfilment of, say, a legal obligation; instead prayer and petition emerge first and foremost as a 'vocation', that of praising the glory of '*Kyrios pantokrator*'.

This act of praise offered by God's people is seen as a sharing in the liturgy celebrated by angelic powers in heaven through the unceasing worship of God's name (Isaiah 6.2–3); and because of this eschatological factor it takes the form of a real concelebration. When we pray that our supplication may be received on the altar of heaven, that altar can only belong to the Apocalypse.

This joyful Eucharist offered to the Lord of the Universe – a theme which is of course a frequent one in the Liturgy of the Hours – owes its existence to the cycle of light and darkness being understood as a gift from God. Darkness is seen not as a time of temptation but as an opportunity to rest and to contemplate spiritual light, while the sun reaching its height is the cue to reflect on God's radiant majesty.

The first light of dawn and the evening twilight are equally symbolic of the spiritual light of divine revelation through which we have become children of light; and for the catechumens baptism, in the terminology beloved of Patristic thought, is called 'illumination'. This theme, along with the others that underlie various prayers in the *asmatike akolouthia*, is rooted in antiquity, and it is not hard to see in it a clear echo of the Jewish *Berakoth*, especially the *Yozer* that precedes the reciting of the *Shema* 'Hear, O Israel . . .' (Deuteronomy 6.4–9):

> Blessed are you, O Lord our God, King of the universe, who formed the light and created the darkness . . . in your mercy you gave light to the earth and to all who live in it and in your goodness you daily renew your creation . . . Our blessed and omniscient God prepared and formed the sun's rays: a gift he made to the glory of his Name. Blessed are you . . . our King and Redeemer . . . creator of the spirits that serve you . . . in the heights of heaven . . ., they worship, praise and glorify the Name of the great king . . . his Name is Holy! . . . In heavenly music they all respond, saying . . . Holy, Holy, Holy, Lord God of Hosts . . .

The constant use of the word 'Remember . . .' also points us in the same direction. The remembrance or *memorial* (*zikkaron*) of salvation that is offered to God along with our requests, as a genuine sacrifice, expresses the certainty that God's saving intervention in the past retains all its dynamic power in the present.

Not surprisingly, because of this dependence on Jewish models, there is not a reference to the mediation of Christ in the final doxology to every prayer in the *euchologion*.

The Liturgy of the Hours of the 'Great Church', apart from

being a time of prayer, supplication, thanksgiving and obedient recognition of one's own unworthiness, is also a meeting place, where God may respond immediately to human need. The divine *oracle* is expressed in the final prayer of blessing at the end of each service, the *kephaloklisia* (= inclination prayer). For the Israelites, 'pronouncing the Name of the divinity over the faithful was a guarantee of blessing': for us, 'Yahweh has been replaced by *Kyrios* and the emphasis is not now on the "Name" itself but on God's benevolent watchfulness and the peace that this gives.'

After the Frankish capture of Constantinople in 1204 the whole Byzantine Church gradually adopted the monastic Canonical Hours, the only form still in use today. In these prayers, thanks to the synthesis provided by studies in monasticism, we can see some elements of the ancient *asmatikos* still surviving, and with them about twenty of the president's prayers. These, however, are recited in a low voice, one after the other, some during the introductory psalm at vespers and some during the psalmody before daybreak, if they are not included in other offices. Prayers which were originally composed to be heard by everyone are now said privately by the clergy in what is often a very hasty recitation.

Churches of the Byzantine tradition should seriously consider the possibility, if not of returning to the old rite, then at least of improving the arrangement of today's rite. This became 'official' only because it was printed, and is no more than the arbitrary selection of an ignorant 16th-century Venetian typographer.